FIVE LAWS
∽ OF THE ∽
DYING
SEED

FIVE LAWS
~ OF THE ~
DYING
SEED

DISCOVER THE SECRET TO A FRUITFUL LIFE

FUCHSIA
PICKETT

Charisma
HOUSE
A STRANG COMPANY

FIVE LAWS OF THE DYING SEED by Fuchsia Pickett
Published by Charisma House
A part of Strang Communications Company
600 Rinehart Road
Lake Mary, Florida 32746
www.charismahouse.com

Unless otherwise noted Scripture quotations are from the
New American Standard Bible. Copyright © 1960, 1962,
1963, 1968, 1971, 1972, 1973, 1975, 1977 by the Lockman
Foundation. Used by permission. (www.Lockman.org)

Scripture quotations marked AMP are from the Amplified
Bible. Old Testament copyright © 1965, 1987 by the
Zondervan Corporation. The Amplified New Testament
copyright © 1954, 1958, 1987 by the Lockman Foundation.
Used by permission.

Scripture quotations marked KJV are from the King James
Version of the Bible.

Cover design by Rachel Campbell
Interior typography by Sallie Traynor

Library of Congress Cataloging-in-Publication Data

Pickett, Fuchsia T.
 Five laws of the dying seed / Fuchsia Pickett.
    p. cm.
 ISBN 0-88419-965-7
 1. Bible. N.T. John XII, 20-26—Criticism, interpreta-
tion, etc. I. Title.
 BS2615.52.P53 2003
 226.5'06—dc21

                    2003007319

03 04 05 06 07 — 87654321
Printed in the United States of America

Truly God's gifts exceed our expectations.
It has been so with His gift to me for the last
fourteen years. He brought to me a true
dedicated friend who has been my "right arm"
during these years. She has come along beside
me in every phase of my life and has become
my daughter in the faith. She is a true friend to
help me in becoming a dying seed, enabling me
to see Jesus with her heart and life as a servant,
friend and colaborer. Joan Gebhardt has
fulfilled a large part of our ministry.

Through her life I've truly seen what the
Word declares a servant of God really is.
I am eternally grateful for the gift of God,
Joan Gebhardt. It is to her
I lovingly dedicate this book.

Contents

3

Now there were certain Greeks among those who were going up to worship at the feast; these therefore came to Philip, who was from Bethsaida of Galilee, and began to ask him, saying, "Sir, we wish to see Jesus." Philip came and told Andrew; Andrew and Philip came, and they told Jesus. And Jesus answered them, saying, "The hour has come for the Son of Man to be glorified. Truly, truly, I say to you, unless a grain of wheat falls into the earth and dies, it remains by itself alone; but if it dies, it bears much fruit. He who loves his life loses it; and he who hates his life in this world shall keep it to life eternal. If anyone serves Me, let him follow Me; and where I am, there shall My servant also be; if anyone serves Me, the Father will honor him."

—JOHN 12:20–26

Introduction

Dear Reader,

Have you seen Jesus? Would you like to? Do you think you have to wait until you get to heaven to look on His lovely face, to enjoy intimate relationship with Him?

In the next few pages, I want to share with you a revelation God gave to me that is filled with promise to satisfy every heart that hungers to see the Master—here and now, not only when heaven's gates swing open for you to enter.

If you are willing to meet the requirements Jesus revealed to those who asked to see Him, you will receive the desire of your heart—in this life as well as in the life to come. It is the Lord's desire that we walk in intimate fellowship with Him who came to reveal the Father to us. I promise you that the Scriptures are true when they declare:

> Things which eye has not seen and ear has not heard, and which have not entered the heart of man, all that God has prepared for those who love Him.
>
> —1 CORINTHIANS 2:9

Why do so many Christians live beneath their privilege and fail to appropriate the promise of God? Jesus reveals the answer to that question in one of His last discourses on earth. As you read, allow the Holy Spirit to open your eyes to the possibilities of a satisfying relationship available to every believer who chooses to follow Jesus.

My prayer is that you will see Him whom your soul loves and allow Him to give you His resurrection life and power, which will bring you complete fulfillment. Then you will be able to give life to others and bear much fruit for eternity.

Chapter 1

RESPONDING TO JESUS

*But one thing is needful: and Mary
hath chosen that good part, which shall
not be taken away from her.*
—LUKE 10:42, KJV

H ave you ever wondered why Jesus answered
people in ways that seemed unrelated to
their comments or questions? I have often read the
Scriptures and wondered why Jesus responded in a
way that seemed only indirectly related—
or entirely unrelated—to the question He had
been asked. For example, when Nicodemus, a ruler
of the Jews, came to Jesus at night, he began his
conversation by acknowledging, "Rabbi, we know
that You have come from God as a teacher; for no
one can do these signs that You do unless God is
with him" (John 3:2). The Bible says that Jesus
answered him:

> Truly, truly, I say to you, unless one is born
> again, he cannot see the kingdom of God.
>   —JOHN 3:3

Jesus' answer to Nicodemus sounds appropriate
only in response to a question regarding what one
must do to enter the kingdom of God, a question
that Nicodemus did not ask. Unless, of course, it
was the real question his heart longed to have
answered, the real reason he came to see Jesus,
which the Master understood.

When the woman at the well asked Jesus to give
her the living water He promised she could have, He
told her to bring her husband to the well. His
response seemed totally irrelevant to her request. As
He led her through the revelatory conversation that
followed, however, she did receive the living water

He had promised her; she saw Jesus as her Messiah and then shared that revelation with her entire community. (See John 4:7–30.)

The Canaanite woman who came to Jesus, begging Him to heal her daughter, at first received no response at all from Him. Then she heard an explanation of Jesus' mission on earth, followed by His rebuke:

> And behold, a Canaanite woman came out from that region, and began to cry out, saying, "Have mercy on me, O Lord, Son of David; my daughter is cruelly demon-possessed." But He did not answer her a word. And His disciples came to Him and kept asking Him, saying, "Send her away, for she is shouting out after us." But He answered and said, "I was sent only to the lost sheep of the house of Israel." But she came and began to bow down before Him, saying, "Lord, help me!" And He answered and said, "It is not good to take the children's bread and throw it to the dogs." But she said, "Yes, Lord; but even the dogs feed on the crumbs which fall from their master's table."
>
> —MATTHEW 15:22–27

Jesus' heart was so touched by this Gentile woman's persistent response, which revealed her faith, that He not only healed her daughter, but also commended her great faith in His lordship (v. 28).

Perhaps part of our difficulty in understanding

Jesus' responses lies in the difference between our Western mind and the Eastern culture of which He was a part. The oriental mind approaches problem solving much differently than we do, and teachers often used stories to teach principles and reveal truths that offer solutions and answers.

For example, when Jesus taught that in order to inherit the kingdom of God we should love our neighbor as we love ourselves, the lawyer responded defensively, trying to justify himself by asking, "And who is my neighbor?" (Luke 10:29). Jesus answered him by telling the familiar story of the

Jesus often answered the real question or desire of the heart from a spiritual perspective, even if the question was asked from a limited human perspective.

good Samaritan to demonstrate the answer to this insincere question.

Another problem we have in understanding Jesus' response is that He often answered the real question or desire of the heart from a spiritual perspective, even if the question was asked from a limited human perspective. I believe this is the problem we have understanding Jesus' response to His disciples in the text from John with which we started this book. When Jesus' disciples told Him that several Greek men had asked to see Him, we encounter another seemingly enigmatic response from Jesus.

The request seems simple—"We wish to see Jesus" (John 12:21). Yet, in answer to their request, Jesus replied, "Unless a grain of wheat falls into the earth and dies, it remains by itself alone" (v. 24).

Was Jesus ignoring the specific request brought to Him by His disciples? Did He just begin to converse with them about what was really on His mind at the time instead of responding to the question presented Him? I think that, inadvertently, we read the Scriptures that way sometimes, failing to understand the connection between the question and the response Jesus gives. We conclude that Jesus didn't respond directly to people but taught them what He wanted them to know instead.

I do not believe that is the case. Jesus never wasted words, and He was keenly interested in meeting the needs of people—especially those whose desire to understand pressed them to seek Him out, as with these Greeks. The Scripture is clear regarding the fact that Jesus was responding to their request when it declares that Jesus *answered* them (v. 23). He didn't ignore them; He answered them. He didn't just teach a lesson; He answered them.

Jesus' response was not even a parable, though He did use an analogy to explain His answer. Instead, He revealed the heart of the matter—He explained clearly what is actually involved when someone wants to see Jesus. He also used the occasion of this question to announce His death. That was not what the disciples expected; they were not expecting to see Him die. Hadn't they just come from a celebration hailing Him as King when Jesus entered Jerusalem riding on a donkey? Surely the next major event in Jesus' life could not be His death.

Did these Greek men gain an audience with the Master? The Scriptures are not clear about their appointment with Him. Did Jesus respond to their request to see Him? Absolutely! And His response not only met the needs of a few Greeks who wanted to see Him, but also it teaches all of mankind how to see Him, regardless of nationality, profession, gender or the

These five spiritual laws of the dying seed provide understanding of the route we are going to have to take if we are to follow Jesus.

age in which we live. Every person who would ever express a desire to see Jesus, to really know Him, received the answer to their quest in Jesus' response that day:

> Truly, truly, I say to you, unless a grain of wheat falls into the earth and dies, it remains by itself alone; but if it dies, it bears much fruit. He who loves his life loses it; and he who hates his life in this world shall keep it to life eternal. If anyone serves Me, let him follow Me; and where I am, there shall My servant

also be; if anyone serves Me, the Father will
honor him.

—JOHN 12:24–26

In Jesus' response, He unfolds five spiritual laws
of the dying seed. These life-giving principles are
not a popular doctrine; they do not fit much of
Charismatic theology. But these spiritual laws provide an understanding of the route we are going to
have to take if we are to follow Jesus in reality,
beholding Him in His death and resurrection and
choosing to live in the same way He did to glorify
the Father.

I don't believe we will have a true revelation of
Jesus without experiencing personally the crucified
life about which Jesus taught us. Knowing the
power of the cross in our lives means following
Jesus on the same path He took—the path He
described in His analogy of the dying seed. Jesus
came to die in order to give eternal life to many,
bearing much fruit for eternity. He knew that His
purpose for coming could only be fulfilled through
His death.

Now My soul has become troubled; and what
shall I say, "Father, save Me from this hour"?
But for this purpose I came to this hour.

—JOHN 12:27

Have you seen Jesus? Would you like to? Are you
prepared to respond to the truth He revealed
through the laws of the dying seed? As you consider

the spiritual laws that Jesus revealed in His response to the Greeks' request to see Him, you will be able to answer these questions. Your answers will determine whether or not you have a genuine desire to see Jesus—to know Him as He desires for you to know Him.

Cutting through every creed, dogma, religious tradition and every kind of pretense, Jesus' discourse reveals the way to see Him. In the simple analogy of the dying seed, He shows how these spiritual laws work irrefutably in the lives of those who would see Him. While they speak of death, these laws are filled with hope, teaching us how to enjoy resurrection life and satisfying fruitfulness as we cultivate a supernatural relationship with the Son of God.

A spiritual law is an irrefutable force that works for good or bad, regardless of any attempt to change it, ignore it, refute it or deny its existence. We often refer to the law of gravity to illustrate this undeniable force in a natural law. Gravity is a force that is unseen yet quite obvious to those who try to work against it—especially to the person who defies it or denies its reality. Spiritual laws are equally unyielding forces that bring consequences, knowingly or unknowingly, to the person who is ignorant of them. They can also bring incredible blessing to the one who is aware of them and who chooses to yield to their supernatural wisdom.

As we examine five spiritual laws revealed in Jesus' analogy of the dying seed, you may discover that,

either through ignorance or neglect, or perhaps in
blatant disobedience to these laws, you are forfeiting
the power of resurrection life as well as fulfillment of
your divine destiny in God. The laws will not change. But if you have a sincere desire to see Jesus and will embrace the understanding of what you must do to fulfill

> *A spiritual law is an irrefutable force that works for good or bad, regardless of any attempt to change it, ignore it, refute it or deny its existence.*

that desire, you can begin to walk in new depths of
relationship with Him.

When you seek to fulfill that desire God placed
in your heart, a desire that expresses itself in the
words "I wish to see Jesus," you will see Jesus in
ways you did not know were possible, and you will
glorify Him in your life. You can even receive honor
from God as the Scriptures declare that Jesus did.
(See John 8:54; 12:26; 2 Peter 1:17.) As you express
your desire to see Jesus, I invite you to open your
heart and mind to the process involved, which
assures you the answer to your heart's desire. As
you choose to embrace the *Five Laws of the Dying
Seed,* you will begin to live a life of wonder and awe
in the unfolding purposes of God for your life—
now and for eternity.

Chapter 2

THE LAW OF
THE TIME ELEMENT

*To every thing there is a season, and a
time to every purpose under the heaven.*
—ECCLESIASTES 3:1, KJV

God does not dwell in time; He dwells in eternity. I like to imagine that in Creation, God split an eon in two and called it time. He made time work for mankind, allowing for days, nights and seasons in order to nurture the purposes for everything He had made. Though God does not dwell in time, He is meticulous in His use of time, setting specific days and hours for the fulfillment of His purposes for mankind's redemption and for the unfolding of His eternal plan throughout the ages.

You have only to read the Scriptures to understand God's accountability for the timing of every divine purpose He has ordained. For example, the wisest man on earth, under the inspiration of the Holy Spirit, declared:

> To every thing there is a season, and a time to every purpose under the heaven: A time to be born, and a time to die; a time to plant, and a time to pluck up that which is planted; a time to kill, and a time to heal; a time to break down, and a time to build up; a time to weep, and a time to laugh; a time to mourn, and a time to dance; a time to cast away stones, and a time to gather stones together; a time to embrace, and a time to refrain from embracing; a time to get, and a time to lose; a time to keep, and a time to cast away; a time to rend, and a time to sew; a time to keep silence, and a time to speak; a time to love, and a time to hate; a time of war, and a time of peace.
> —ECCLESIASTES 3:1–8, KJV

God Works by Purpose

While God does not dwell in time, He created time and operates by purpose—by laws and principles—within the parameters of time. The Bible says, "Many are the plans in a man's heart, but the counsel of the LORD, it will stand" (Prov. 19:21). God lays out principles that govern life. Only as we learn to obey God's laws can we come into what He has ordained us to have. Unfortunately, we have difficulty understanding God's laws and principles many times.

During the three years of our Lord's ministry, He cut straight through the intellect of men who operated in sense knowledge. He understood what the Scriptures teach, that "a natural man does not accept the things of the Spirit of God; for they are foolishness to him, and he cannot understand them, because they are spiritually appraised" (1 Cor. 2:14–15). He also challenged the carnal mind, which the Scriptures declare is "enmity against God: for it is not subject to the law of God, neither indeed can be" (Rom. 8:7, KJV).

> *God does not dwell in time; He dwells in eternity.*

When Jesus revealed God's principles, He knew that they could not be understood by our rebellious minds. Yet, He spoke truth in answer to the Greeks' request. His response to them that day was not a carnal statement; it is a spiritual law. Only as we recognize the principle that Jesus was teaching can we understand His response. Jesus' message of the dying seed revealed the reality of the cross. As we choose to embrace the cross as He did, the Holy Spirit pierces the carnality of our minds, and we enter into revelation of God's purposes. He changes our natural thinking into revelation knowledge of the purposes of God in bringing Jesus to earth to make our redemption possible.

We cannot study here the intricate detail with which God planned the redemption of mankind, culminating in the coming of His Son. The Old Testament is filled with the foreshadowing of His coming, revealed in the types and shadows of the ceremonial feasts and offerings faithfully instituted by the Jewish nation. It is fascinating to watch the Scriptures unfold to us the promised Lamb of God according to that divine timetable. Christ became our Passover Lamb, the Spotless One, at the time the ceremonial lamb was to be slain on that terrible day of His crucifixion.

The apostle Paul received revelation of God's purposes, which were ordained from eternity to be introduced at the perfect time. He wrote:

> But when the fulness of the time came, God sent forth His Son, born of a woman, born under the Law, in order that He might redeem those who were under the Law, that

we might receive the adoption as sons.
—GALATIANS 4:4–5

The psalmist understood God's providential involvement in time when he declared, "My times are in Thy hand" (Ps. 31:15). And again, describing the life of Joseph, he wrote, "Until the time that his word came to pass, the word of the LORD tested him [Joseph]" (Ps. 105:19). He even found the boldness to declare to God, "It is time for thee, LORD, to work: for they have made void thy law" (Ps. 119:126, KJV). Understanding that an infinite God has willingly submitted His plan of redemption to the limitation of the time element in which mankind must function is a revelation of the great love God has for His creation. In His omniscient wisdom, God uses time for His eternal purposes.

> *God uses time for His eternal purposes.*

The writer to the Hebrews refers to the time element involved in bringing Christ to earth:

> God, who at sundry times and in divers manners spake in time past unto the fathers by the prophets, hath in these last days spoken unto us by his Son, whom he hath appointed heir of all things, by whom also he made the worlds.
> —HEBREWS 1:1–2, KJV

When Jesus declared in John 12:23 that "the hour has come for the Son of Man to be glorified,"

He recognized that this was the moment for which He had been sent from heaven to earth, from eternity into time, to redeem fallen mankind. Through that redemption, God made it possible for mankind to return from time to eternity, living at home with God forever. Had Jesus not recognized His hour, or if He had chosen to avoid it, His mission would have been thwarted. Jesus understood this terrible possibility of failure when He wept over Jerusalem because it did not recognize the time of its visitation:

> And when He approached [Jerusalem], He saw the city and wept over it, saying, "If you had known in this day, even you, the things which make for peace! But now they have been hidden from your eyes. For the days shall come upon you when your enemies will throw up a bank before you, and surround you, and hem you in on every side, and will level you to the ground and your children within you, and they will not leave in you one stone upon another, because you did not recognize the time of your visitation."
>
> —LUKE 19:41–44

The spiritual law that involves surrendering to the *time element* is necessary for the fulfillment of the purposes of God in your life. It is a necessary principle that, when working in synergy with other divine laws, allows the purposes of God to be fulfilled in a life, in a church, in a nation and throughout the body of Christ. While it cannot stand alone, but works in tandem with other spiritual laws, this law of the time element is always a part of God's process that unfolds His will and work in your life. As you explore the spiritual laws that govern fruitfulness and personal fulfillment, you have to be willing to reckon with the time element that is crucial to your success.

As a little girl, I loved flowers. I still do. But I don't like to wait for them to grow. If I plant the seeds today, I want to pick flowers tomorrow. When I was a girl my mother would help me plant the flower seeds. She showed me the picture of what they would look like. We buried each precious seed and watered the earth around it. Then we waited. Within three days, if the seed had not sprouted, I went out and dug in the ground to find out why. I thought something was wrong with the seed because it wasn't making my flowers in that short time. In my impatience, I aborted the process of planting that seed and allowing the time element to bring my flowers in the proper time.

> *The law of the time element is always a part of God's process that unfolds His will and work in your life.*

The time element works in your life, if you yield to it, to prepare you for the destiny God has for you. It saves you from aborting the work of God in your life, thinking that you know what He wants you to do and then attempting to do it in your own strength out of God's providential time. When you are impatient, you don't give God time to develop His purposes in your life.

The psalmist had learned to trust God with his life. He declared, "My times are in Thy hand; deliver me from the hand of my enemies, and from those who persecute me" (Ps. 31:15). We witness this same trust in Jesus as He came to earth in the fullness of time and walked in perfect submission to His Father toward the fulfillment of all Scripture regarding His death and resurrection.

"MY HOUR HAS COME"

It is undeniable that Jesus was referring to Himself and His imminent death when He used the analogy of the dying seed. He was that seed, abiding alone, until He allowed Himself to fall into the ground and die. This was true in spite of the fact that He lived in perfect communion with His Father, doing the works that He saw the Father do and revealing the very nature of God the Father to mankind. (See John 5:19; 14:9.)

It was true in spite of the miracles and healings Jesus had performed, the multitudes He had taught and the disciples He had chosen to follow Him. He was still alone—a seed in which life dwelt so abundantly that it would be enough to bring every person to God if they chose to receive that life. It…He…the Seed…had only to die.

The prophet Isaiah had foreseen this reality hundreds of years earlier when he declared one of the great messianic prophecies that revealed the suffering of our Lord:

> But the LORD was pleased to crush Him, putting Him to grief; if He would render Himself as a guilt offering, He will see His offspring, He will prolong His days, and the good pleasure of the LORD will prosper in His hand. As a result of the anguish of His soul, He will see it and be satisfied; by His knowledge the Righteous One, My Servant, will justify the many, as He will bear their iniquities.
>
> —ISAIAH 53:10–11

The time element for Jesus to fulfill His divine purpose involved not only His coming to earth and living a sinless life among us, doing the will of the Father. It also involved the hour when that life would be crushed in order to bring redemption from sin for all mankind and to release the resurrection power of God that could be imparted to every sinner, enabling him or her to become a son of God.

Here we see the synergy of two spiritual laws—the law of the *time element* and the law of *death* (which we will discuss in the next chapter)—working together on the "Seed" to bring forth resurrection life. The way to fruitfulness and fulfillment of divine purposes involves this synergy of spiritual laws to which we must submit.

Let's observe the events that surrounded Jesus'

response to the Greeks as His life was coming to a dramatic end, leading Him to Calvary a few days later.

Jesus' Last Days on Earth

The time element of events that surrounded Jesus' response to the Greeks who came to see Him centered in the last days of His life on earth before His crucifixion. They were exciting days, filled with meaningful happenings for blessing as well as cursing.

Anointed for burial

The Scriptures tell us that six days before the Passover feast, which Jesus would celebrate with His disciples, He went to His friends' house in Bethany—the home of Mary, Martha and Lazarus, whom Jesus had raised from the dead. It was during this supper that Mary took a very costly perfume and began to anoint the feet of Jesus and wipe them with her hair. (See John 12:1–3.) When Judas complained that such a costly perfume was being wasted in that way, Jesus warned, "Let her alone, in order that she may keep it for the day of My burial" (v. 7).

> *The way to fruitfulness and fulfillment of divine purposes involves the synergy of spiritual laws to which we must submit.*

This blessed event for Jesus seemed to be a catalyst

for Judas to continue his plans to betray the Master, as the writer of the Gospel of John took the time to reveal Judas's motivation for his complaint, that he was a thief. He also added that Judas was intending to betray Jesus. Plans must have been in the making for that heinous deed at that time, because a few days later they were carried out, resulting in the mock trial that Jesus endured and, ultimately, His crucifixion.

Large crowds were following Jesus during those days, not just to see Jesus but also to see Lazarus, the man who had returned from the grave when Jesus raised him from the dead. Such an astonishing miracle was worthy of a long, dusty walk to be an eyewitness, and many Jews were anxious to do just that. It was so frustrating to the religious leaders of the day that they "took counsel that they might put Lazarus to death" as well as Jesus in order to put an end to their "competition" and bring order back to their religious domain (vv. 9–11).

Triumphal entry

It was the next day, according to Scripture, after His dinner with His friends, that Jesus walked to Jerusalem. When the news spread that Jesus was coming, a huge crowd of people who were in Jerusalem to celebrate the Passover took branches of palm trees and went out to meet Him, shouting "Hosanna! Blessed is He who comes in the name of the Lord, even the King of Israel" (John 12:13).

Jesus, who had intentionally escaped earlier

attempts of the people to make Him king, knew that it was His time to be recognized as King of the Jews, fulfilling many Old Testament prophecies and allowing God to be glorified in His life in that way. He also knew that this triumphal entrance into Jerusalem was only a precursor to the terrible death that awaited Him, which was also to be reckoned with in "this hour."

Bible scholars believe it was a day or two after Jesus' triumphal entry into Jerusalem that the incident occurred when several Greeks asked to have a meeting with Him.[1] They came respectfully trying to gain a private audience with Jesus, obviously to converse with Him.

It is significant that of all the events that could have been recorded about the last days of Jesus, the request of these Greeks is included in the Scriptures. Perhaps it was not so much their request as it was Jesus' response that was necessary to be preserved for all believers to understand. Through Jesus' response He revealed eternal truths regarding resurrection life, fruitfulness and discipleship that are crucial to our spiritual journey.

Gentile believers?

We know from history that there were people from Gentile nations who worshiped the God of the Jews; even the temple structure gave them a place to worship, though with limited access. Matthew Henry comments that part of the significance of this incident is its promise of the wonderful act of redemption that was about to occur, which would tear the veil from the temple, allowing both Jews and Gentiles to experience the salvation for which they longed.[2] These Greeks were a kind of prototype of all Gentiles who would soon be able to come with the same request, "We wish to see Jesus."

> Jesus revealed the overriding destiny for each life—to bring glory to the Father.

While the Greeks become incidental to the words of Jesus in response to their inquiry, we have them to thank for initiating the short analogy and one of Jesus' last discourses, which gives us so much insight into the laws of redemption. There are several main themes that we can discern from Jesus' words and at least five laws of redemption that we can apply to our lives. One of the themes is the goal of bringing glory to the Father. In declaring that goal, Jesus revealed the overriding destiny for each life—to bring glory to the Father. We do that when we learn to bear much fruit in the way the dying seed would do.

This theme of the dying seed is reminiscent of another analogy, or parable, that Jesus told of the sower who went out to sow his seed:

> And when a great multitude were coming together, and those from the various cities were journeying to Him, He spoke by way of a

parable: "The sower went out to sow his seed; and as he sowed, some fell beside the road; and it was trampled under foot, and the birds of the air ate it up. And other seed fell on rocky soil, and as soon as it grew up, it withered away, because it had no moisture. And other seed fell among the thorns; and the thorns grew up with it, and choked it out. And other seed fell into the good soil, and grew up, and produced a crop a hundred times as great." As He said these things, He would call out, "He who has ears to hear, let him hear."

—LUKE 8:4–8

When His disciples failed once more to understand the teaching of the Lord, Jesus patiently explained it to them:

Now the parable is this: the seed is the word of God. And those beside the road are those who have heard; then the devil comes and takes away the word from their heart, so that they may not believe and be saved. And those on the rocky soil are those who, when they hear, receive the word with joy; and these have no firm root; they believe for a while, and in time of temptation fall away. And the seed which fell among the thorns, these are the ones who have heard, and as they go on their way they are choked with worries and riches and pleasures of this life, and bring no fruit to maturity. And the seed in the good soil, these are the ones who have heard the word in an honest and

good heart, and hold it fast, and bear fruit with
perseverance.

—LUKE 8:11–15

In this parable, Jesus explains that the seed is the
Word of God. There is an interesting correlation
between this parable and the analogy of the dying
seed. We have said that Jesus was referring to
Himself as the seed that must fall into the ground
and die in that analogy. When we look at the beginning of John's Gospel, we understand that Jesus is
the living Word of God, the Seed that was sown to
bring forth fruit:

> In the beginning was the Word, and the
> Word was with God, and the Word was God
> …And the Word became flesh, and dwelt
> among us, and we beheld His glory, glory as
> of the only begotten from the Father, full of
> grace and truth.
>
> —JOHN 1:1, 14

The Scriptures refer to Jesus as the Word of God
as well as the Seed that would bruise the serpent's
head. (See Genesis 3:15.) To fulfill the plan of
redemption, the Word of heaven had to become the
Son of God, Jesus, on earth. He was filled with the
glory of God, and He would be glorified again
through His death on the cross. As the living Word,
Jesus knew He was the Seed that would bruise the
serpent's head in order to buy back the human race
so we could become the family of God.

While we may never grasp the magnitude of God becoming man—the Son of God leaving eternity to enter time—we can understand that there was a perfect time for Him to come. And the time element played out in every moment of His life and ultimately led Him to His death. The apostle Paul referred to this time element in the life of Christ when he declared, "For when we were yet without strength, in *due time* Christ died for the ungodly" (Rom. 5:6, KJV, emphasis added).

Paul further explained that time was not to be valued over the glory that would be produced as a result: "For I reckon that the sufferings of this *present time* are not worthy to be compared with the glory which shall be revealed in us" (Rom. 8:18, KJV, emphasis added). When he spoke of the *due time* of Christ's death and the *present time* of our sufferings, he was acknowledging the law of the time element that is necessary to bring forth eternal glory. This law is only a tool in the hand of God to produce eternal reward.

> *While we may never grasp the magnitude of God becoming man, we can understand that there was a perfect time for Him to come.*

When we study the lives of Bible heroes, we can readily understand the role that this spiritual law played in their destinies. Their lives were played out on the stage of time; yet as they sought to know God, their journeys rewarded them with fruitfulness that was eternal.

ABRAHAM'S PERPLEXING PROMISE

While we cannot trace the complete course of Abraham, the patriarch of our faith, it may be helpful to point out how he was tested by God through the element of time. God had promised Abraham an heir out of his and Sarah's union, promising as well that their seed would be "as the dust of the earth" (Gen. 13:16).

Yet, after Abraham and Sarah were old, they still did not have the promised son. So Sarah convinced Abraham to overrule the providential time element and bring God's promise to pass by having a son by Hagar, her handmaid. You are familiar with the story of how Hagar gave birth to Ishmael, the son of Abraham. But God was not concerned with the thwarted time element, the aging bodies of Sarah and Abraham, or the barrenness of Sarah. He intended to fulfill His promise in His time, when He could get the most glory, in spite of the perplexity it was causing His friend, Abraham. And in God's time, Sarah did conceive the son of Abraham—the promised son, Isaac—after the testing of their faith through the law of the time element.

MOSES' WILDERNESS WANDERING

Not many Christians are excited about signing up for the wilderness sojourn that was required of Moses before he was to become the deliverer of God's people. For forty years Moses tended sheep on the backside of the desert, alienated from his people and from the comfortable lifestyle to which he had grown accustomed in Pharaoh's palace. Banished by his own violent actions—the murder of an Egyptian—Moses could have blamed himself for his plight.

> *The law of the time element is only a tool in the hand of God to produce eternal reward.*

Yet, regardless of the circumstances, God was simply using the law of the time element to prepare His chosen deliverer to lead the Israelites out of bondage. Have you ever wondered why the New Testament seems so kind to Moses when referring to his personal wilderness season? It simply records Moses as a hero of faith:

> By faith Moses, when he had grown up, refused to be called the son of Pharaoh's daughter; choosing rather to endure ill-treatment with the people of God, than to enjoy the passing pleasures of sin; considering the reproach of Christ greater riches than the treasures of Egypt; for he was looking to the reward.
>
> —HEBREWS 11:24–26

The transforming power that worked in Moses' heart during those forty years on the backside of the desert prepared him to bring glory to God by delivering His people from slavery. And it prepared Moses to behold the glory of God, perhaps in a way no man had ever beheld Him before. Wasted years? Years of defeat? Years of darkness? Perhaps. But these years were undoubtedly redeemed by the power of God to bring forth much fruit for eternity.

> *God intends to fulfill His promise in His time, when He can get the most glory.*

We live in a world of fast food, instant credit and high-speed Internet, which gives us expectations that we can have what we want when we want it—*now*! However, this mentality does not bring results in the kingdom of God. We must submit to the law of the time element if we expect to fulfill the eternal destiny that God has ordained for us.

JOSEPH'S JOURNEY

Perhaps Joseph's journey parallels more closely the journey of Jesus than any other Bible hero. The favorite son of his father, Joseph was exiled from his homeland, betrayed and sold by his brothers, which required him to live his life in a foreign land. The blessing of God was on his life, and even his pagan owners could see that God was with him. Yet, his righteous life was maligned once again by his owner's wife, and Joseph was thrown into prison. Even there it was apparent that God was with him, and he was given responsibility for the prison.

It is the psalmist who gives us insight into the *pain* of the time element that Joseph experienced:

> He sent a man before them,
> Joseph, who was sold as a slave.
> They afflicted his feet with fetters,
> He himself was laid in irons;
> Until the time that his word came to pass,
> The word of the Lord tested him.
> The king sent and released him,
> The ruler of peoples, and set him free.
> He made him lord of his house,
> And ruler over all his possessions,
> To imprison his princes at will,
> That he might teach his elders wisdom.
>
> —Psalm 105:17–22

The word of the Lord tested Joseph until the time that it came to pass. What was that word? Joseph had dreamed that his brothers would bow down to him and that even his father would pay him homage. Yet, he was exiled from his homeland and family and was imprisoned in a foreign land.

PAUL'S PERSONAL PREPARATION

For the struggling young church enduring heavy persecution, perhaps one of the most significant and encouraging events was the conversion of Saul, who had killed and imprisoned many Christians. Saul, whose name the Lord changed to Paul, was extremely educated in religious matters, and after his conversion, he found it exhilarating to prove the reality of Christ's redemption from the Scriptures he had misinterpreted earlier.

Yet, almost without comment, God whisked His newly converted apostle away to Arabia where, for at least three years, Paul allowed the law of the time element to do its transforming work in his mind and heart as well as in his theology. We may never know the extent of that work, which undoubtedly prepared the apostle Paul for the writing of much of the New Testament, as well as the courage it took to bear the burden of the churches and suffer the physical persecution and imprisonment that characterized his life.

> *We must submit to the law of the time element if we expect to fulfill the eternal destiny that God has ordained for us.*

Perhaps largely because of that personal preparation, he could speak disdainfully of the "sufferings of this present time [that] are not worthy to be compared with the glory that is to be revealed to us" (Rom. 8:18). Certainly the relationship he had cultivated with the Master caused him to "desire to depart [this life] and be with Christ, for that is very much better" (Phil. 1:23). And his intense passion to know Christ above all else was abundantly clear.

> I count all things to be loss in view of the sur-
> passing value of knowing Christ Jesus my
> Lord, for whom I have suffered the loss of all
> things, and count them but rubbish in order
> that I may gain Christ, and may be found in
> Him, not having a righteousness of my own
> derived from the Law, but that which is
> through faith in Christ, the righteousness
> which comes from God on the basis of faith,
> that I may know Him, and the power of His
> resurrection and the fellowship of His suffer-
> ings, being conformed to His death.
>
> —PHILIPPIANS 3:8–10

And so we come to the second spiritual law of the
dying seed—the law of death. The apostle Paul
expressed his passion to gain Christ, much like the
Greeks who went to great lengths to see Jesus. He
had willingly suffered the loss of all things in order
to gain Christ. His desire was not just to know the
power of Christ's resurrection and enter into the fellowship of His sufferings, but to be conformed to
His death as well.

Do you desire to see Jesus in spite of the suffering
and death it may require? That was the passion of the
apostle Paul and of countless martyrs throughout
history who despised this life when compared to the
faith they had found in Christ. Here we enter into a
spiritual law that will test our hearts like no other.

As we have stated, the law of the time element
does not stand alone, unrelated to the other spiritual

laws that are involved in making us fruitful and
allowing us to know the resurrection power that the
apostle Paul knew. However, it is important that we
understand how crucial it is to the redemption
process. Without it, there can be no process; it takes
time to die.

God ordained the use of the time element to fulfill His eternal purposes for each one of His children.

*Without the law of the
time element, there can
be no process; it take
time to die.*

As we consider the next
spiritual law involved
in the process of attain-
ing resurrection life, we
will understand more
clearly how the time
element works its will
on the "dying seed."
May our hearts grasp
the depths of life it offers to us under the guise of
sacrificial death.

Chapter 3

THE LAW
OF DEATH

*Truly, truly, I say to you, unless a grain
of wheat falls into the earth and dies, it
remains by itself alone; but if it dies,
it bears much fruit.*

—JOHN 12:24

When Jesus declared, "The hour has come for the Son of Man to be glorified," He was announcing the fact of His imminent death (John 12:23). Jesus understood that His death was necessary to glorify the Father, as we have mentioned. That is clear from Jesus' prayer that followed: "Father, glorify Thy name" (v. 28). This prayer brought an audible response from the throne of God. The Father replied, "I have both glorified it, and will glorify it again" (v. 28). Everything Jesus did while He lived on earth honored the Father, revealing the Father's character and nature to fallen humanity. And in Jesus' death, God would again receive the glory, honor and worshipful praise that He deserves.

While we may have difficulty relating to the term *glorified* as Jesus used it referring to His death, we can understand from His statements that Jesus knew it was necessary for Him to die in order to be glorified. The Greek word for *glorify* that Jesus used is *doxazo*, which means "to make glorious, to be full of glory, to honor and magnify."[1] Jesus knew that in going to the cross, He would bring glory (honor, praise and worship) to the Father. He understood that He must become that Seed that falls into the ground and dies in order to bring forth much fruit.

> *Jesus' death would open the way for all nations to come to God.*

How does this declaration relate to the disciples'
message from the Greeks who were requesting to
see Him? Jesus was saying that these men would
indeed see Him as He was lifted up on the cross. He
declared in this same discourse, "And I, if I be lifted
up from the earth, will draw all men to Myself"
(v. 32). Jesus' death would open the way for all
nations to come to God. These Greeks would not
only see Him in His death, but they also would be
ushered into His kingdom through His resurrection, when the way was opened to all men, if they
chose to follow Him.

The apostle Paul explains the hopeless plight of
Gentiles before Christ's atonement, which included
them:

> Wherefore remember, that ye being in time
> past Gentiles in the flesh, who are called
> Uncircumcision by that which is called the
> Circumcision in the flesh made by hands; that
> at that time ye were without Christ, being
> aliens from the commonwealth of Israel, and
> strangers from the covenants of promise, hav-
> ing no hope, and without God in the world:
> But now in Christ Jesus ye who sometimes
> were far off are made nigh by the blood of
> Christ. For he is our peace, who hath made
> both one, and hath broken down the middle
> wall of partition between us...And came and
> preached peace to you which were afar off,
> and to them that were nigh.
>
> —EPHESIANS 2:11–14, 17, KJV

Jesus' response to His disciples and to the Greeks' request did not only point them to the cross and His own death, but it also revealed what was required of any man who would see Jesus and who desires to glorify God by bearing much fruit:

> Truly, truly, I say to you, unless a grain of wheat falls into the earth and dies, it remains by itself alone; but if it dies, it bears much fruit.
>
> —JOHN 12:24

These Greeks were fulfilling the first requirement to see Jesus—that of the time element. Their priority was to get to Jesus, and they had pressed into the inner circle of people, appealing to His disciples to get them an audience with Him. Jesus was explaining the next requirement for them to see Him—they would have to die. He did not mean they had to die as He was going to do on the cross; nevertheless, they would have to die to their own lives in order to follow Him:

> He who loves his life loses it; and he who hates his life in this world shall keep it to life eternal. If anyone serves Me, let him follow Me; and where I am, there shall My servant also be; if anyone serves Me, the Father will honor him.
>
> —JOHN 12:25–26

Let me state clearly that Jesus' message is not a message of death; it is a message of abundant life. He knew that death was the pathway, but His goal was resurrection life—not only for Himself, but for us as well. In my sixty years of ministry I have witnessed churches and sometimes entire movements that emphasize the "death to self" message to such an extent that it seems all of life is about dying. They never experience the joy and fulfillment of resurrection life, which is the goal of death to our natural, soulish life. That was not the message of Christ.

Jesus was simply explaining that resurrection life comes out of losing our lives. He wanted us to understand that out of death comes life and that without death there is no life. His message focused on the antithesis of death—resurrection life that would glorify God alone. Yet, it underscored the necessity of death, a spiritual law that we must embrace if we are to become fruitful in the kingdom of God.

> Jesus' message is not a message of death; it is a message of abundant life.

When Jesus declared that "he who loves his life loses it; and he who hates his life in this world shall keep it to life eternal" (John 12:25), He was using two different Greek words for *life*. Understanding the difference between these two words has helped me to understand the law of death. The life we are to give up is *psuche*, the natural life we live without God.[2] And the life we gain is *zoe*, the everlasting, perpetual life that lives with God.[3] Jesus was teaching that we have to become unconcerned for our earthly life, even despising it, in order to pursue the life of God—everlasting life—that makes us fruitful and causes us to bring glory to God. Another Scripture passage clarifies this:

> If anyone intends to come after Me, let him deny himself [forget, ignore, disown, and lose sight of himself and his own interests] and take up his cross, and [joining Me as a disciple and siding with My party] follow with Me [continually, cleaving steadfastly to Me]. For whoever wants to save his [higher, spiritual, eternal] life, will lose it [the lower, natural, temporal life which is lived only on earth]; and whoever gives up his life [which is lived only on earth] for My sake and the Gospel's will save it [his higher, spiritual life in the eternal kingdom of God].
>
> —MARK 8:34–35, AMP

It is striking that after three and one-half years of ministry—during which Jesus performed many healings and miracles, feeding thousands supernaturally, calming storms and teaching people to know God—He defined fruitfulness in a completely different way. We would probably consider anyone who did all the supernatural signs and wonders that Jesus did to have a very fruitful life. Yet, when Jesus announced His death, He declared that unless a seed falls into the ground and dies, it abides alone. But if it died, it would bring forth much fruit. Jesus would become fruitful through His death.

In that statement, Jesus identified fruit for us. Fruit is a life that brings forth more life; it is not miracles or signs and wonders. It is not simply obedience to the commands of the Father, which Jesus had fulfilled perfectly, resulting in eternal reward. Fruit is resurrection life that emanates from a seed that has yielded completely to the process of death. This understanding can help us to grasp the true meaning of the fruit of the Spirit that the apostle Paul described to the Galatians:

Resurrection life comes out of losing our lives.

> But the fruit of the Spirit is love, joy, peace, patience, kindness, goodness, faithfulness, gentleness, self-control; against such things there is no law.
>
> —GALATIANS 5:22–23

He is describing a life that has died to its own interests and selfishness, a life that has surrendered to the lordship of Christ and given up its claims to its own agenda. When we choose to embrace the laws of the dying seed, the laws that guarantee our fruitfulness, there is no law against those qualities of life, according to the Scriptures. This is the life that brings glory to God and enters into the blessings of everlasting life here on earth. It is this life that fulfills its divine destiny and truly sees Jesus.

In that way we experience the promise of "Christ in you, the hope of glory" (Col. 1:27).

DEATH OF A SEED

Let your mind dwell on the wonder of this divine resurrection life while we consider the struggles of that tiny, dying seed. Imagine yourself as a tiny, insignificant seed, placed under an inch of soil—alone. You feel the pressure of a hand that is pressing you into that soil so that no air or light can possibly reach you. It is a frightening, lonely feeling there. You feel weak and helpless, with no way of escaping that dark, damp earth.

Only a few moments ago you were part of a bag full of seeds just like yourself; you were jostling around and visiting with your neighbors. It was warm and comfortable in that bag, and you enjoyed the idea that you were a seed with life inside your shell that was worth something—at least as much as the seeds next to you. It was great to talk about what you would become in life.

Now, it seems that death is imminent. As the days pass and the damp, dark earth closes around you, you feel the hard, round shell that you had polished and taken pride in begin to wither. Oh, no, how could this happen? What will become of you? That is all you have ever known—a perfect, shiny, hard shell that rubbed against other seeds just like yourself. You grow weaker and weaker, and soon there is actually a tear in that shell. The end is very near. No longer can you relate to the "you" that you have always known.

Weaker now, you feel a strong push to the bottom of your shell. What could it be? And then, another push upward from the remnant of your shell. Surely you are dead—how can this be? You feel you are part of the pushing downward and the pushing upward. Now, you can almost see yourself—that is, your shell, just lying there, loose, and yet you are moving upward and downward—and suddenly, what is this? Warmth. Sunlight. You have left the earthen grave and are lifting...what? Leaves? A stem? You think to yourself, *So this is the life that was inside of me all the time. I don't recognize myself. What have I become?*

And the young plant continues to develop, forgetting the shell that is decaying underground, though still not useless. It has simply become food for the new life of the plant. More leaves and more growth appear, and then, wonder of all wonders, there is a different kind of growth, different from the leaves and stem. This must be...it is...*fruit.*

Fruit is resurrection life that emanates from a seed that has yielded completely to the process of death.

And the fruit looks like the seed that went into the ground, only there are dozens of them filled with life themselves.

Jesus understood the law of the harvest, as we

have mentioned. And the prophet Isaiah did foresee the fruit of Jesus' death and resurrection, when he declared:

> Yet it pleased the LORD to bruise him; he hath put him to grief: when thou shalt make his soul an offering for sin, he shall see his seed, he shall prolong his days, and the pleasure of the LORD shall prosper in his hand. He shall see of the travail of his soul, and shall be satisfied: by his knowledge shall my righteous servant justify many; for he shall bear their iniquities.
>
> —ISAIAH 53:10–11, KJV

Jesus was willing to become a dying seed so that He could justify many and be the firstborn among many sons. (See Romans 8:29.) Of course, His death was redemptive in a way that our death to self is not. He was the sinless Son of God, fulfilling the plan of salvation for all of mankind. Yet, when we choose to follow Jesus, embracing the law of death, and begin to bring forth fruit for eternity, we experience the resurrection life and power of Jesus.

Too often we want an easier way. We want people to lay hands on us and pray, expecting that by prayer we can instantly kill our carnality; we call it *deliverance*. For example, we want to be delivered from a demon of impatience and become gentle and patient in a moment. My Bible says, "Tribulation worketh patience" (Rom. 5:3, KJV). That means that patience requires time to work through the difficulties we face. Dying to our impatience cannot happen by the laying on of hands in prayer. We are not delivered from the works of the flesh by the laying on of hands; we are delivered by dying to the flesh and becoming Jesus' disciple, which we will discuss later.

As we submit to the death of our carnal nature, we learn what Scripture means when it declares, "Christ in you, the hope of glory" (Col. 1:27). The resurrection life that flows out of us is the life of God, for which we have deposited the "seed" of our natural life on earth, with all of its carnality and

When we choose to follow Jesus, embracing the law of death, we experience His resurrection life and power.

Adamic nature. When you think about it, it's not much of an exchange. This resurrection life takes on the character of the "rivers of living water" that flow out of our bellies, of which Jesus spoke in John 7:38, bringing life to others as it overflows our own lives.

Until we are willing to become broken, confused, bewildered, helpless and brokenhearted in that place of death to which we yield, we will be egotists who build our lives around our own image—the beautiful seed. Unless you are willing to experience the discomfort of being buried out of sight—where no one shouts your praises or honors you, unrecognized, with your name being forgotten and left out of the awards—you will abide alone.

Remember, there is a time element involved in this process; it takes time to die. When you sense that you are in a situation that is "burying" your carnal nature, if you allow yourself to be "dug up" too soon, you will not know the resurrection life that awaits. Without identity, cut off from everyone, enduring the pressure of the earth as the storms, wind and rain bear upon you, you feel totally ignored—alone. Perhaps it is difficult in those circumstances to believe that a merciful and loving Father arranged it—and that He was responding to your desire, your prayer, to be fruitful and bring Him glory.

He knows what to do with His seed—whether it takes one month, two months, three months or even longer. You may even ask, "Am I ever going to get out of here?" Of course, you are; that is why He is hiding you, to crack the outer lobe, the flesh, off of the precious life He is developing inside. That life will push up through the dark earth and reach for the sunshine. And it will not stop until it brings forth much fruit.

It seems tragic that for some seeds to germinate, the extreme rigors of winter have to exert their pressure—cold winds, freezing weather, rain, ice. The seed has to endure this winter season during which it feels it has no identity; it is cut off from everyone and every source of comfort. Can you hear it whining, "Can't He be merciful and bring me up tomorrow?" The answer is *no*. This process requires time. The seed will not burst forth in resurrection life without the storms, pressure, wind and rain.

It is actually the merciful, loving Father who arranged for your misery, because if you had stayed inside the shell, you would have died without hope of resurrection life. The potential for life within you would never have come forth. Being buried is one of the laws of the harvest, and Christ is the great Husbandman:

> *We are not delivered from the works of the flesh by the laying on of hands; we are delivered by dying to the flesh.*

> Be patient therefore, brethren, unto the coming of the Lord. Behold, the husbandman waiteth for the precious fruit of the earth, and hath long patience for it, until he receive the early and latter rain.
>
> —JAMES 5:7, KJV

After enough pressure, enough storms and enough cold weather—suffering rejection, being ignored while no one seems to care, shivering in the dark, cold earth while others are in the house where it is warm—your shell will begin to shrivel as you prepare both to die and to spring forth into resurrection life.

The Master Gardener knows that it is not time for you to be seen yet. Part of you has to be lost before you burst out of the ground. The lobe or crust around the seed is not the life He ordained for you. It was only carrying the life, protecting it until it could be exposed to the right elements that would bring death to the lobe and release the life He ordained for you from eternity. The life that bursts out of that lobe and pushes up out of the ground is not the seed that went down. When you were buried, you were an old brown seed. You didn't even look like there was life in you. Into the ground you went, and you stayed long enough until the elements began to split the outer crust of the seed, which now is only good for fertilizer to feed the new life that is coming forth.

The body of Christ desperately needs to hear Jesus' message of the dying seed. The day is over that flesh can show off—it now needs to become fertilizer. The life that comes up from the ground is the precious life that the lobe took into the ground. God has placed His divine life in you, and He wants it to come forth. In order for that to happen, He has to get rid of your "natural" man to do it. When you lose that life, you will find your everlasting life, and then the "lobe" of your life turns out to be a blessing.

When the apostle Paul declared that His goal

was to know Christ and the fellowship of His sufferings, he first said that he had *counted* all things
as loss. Then he said that he *suffered* the loss of all
things that he might gain Christ (Phil. 3:7–10).

The day is over that flesh can show off— it now needs to become fertilizer.

I visualize the count-
ing of things as loss
by taking a sheet of
paper and drawing a
line down the middle
to create a ledger. On
the left side, the head-
ing is "Assets," where
you list all of your
assets. The right side of the page is titled "Loss."
The apostle Paul listed his assets:

> Though I might also have confidence in the
> flesh. If any other man thinketh that he hath
> whereof he might trust in the flesh, I more:
> Circumcised the eighth day, of the stock of
> Israel, of the tribe of Benjamin, an Hebrew
> of the Hebrews; as touching the law, a
> Pharisee; concerning zeal, persecuting the
> church; touching the righteousness which is
> in the law, blameless. But what things were
> gain to me, those I counted loss for Christ.
> Yea doubtless, and I count all things but loss
> for the excellency of the knowledge of Christ
> Jesus my Lord: for whom I have suffered the
> loss of all things, and do count them but
> dung, that I may win Christ.
> —PHILIPPIANS 3:4–8, KJV

When you have listed your assets and have decided to count them as loss, it will be the Lord who transfers them to the other column—the loss column. When that happens, you suffer the loss of all things in order to win Christ. If you will start counting things loss, God will enable you to transfer them to the loss column. We don't bring forth fruit by *counting* things loss; we bring forth fruit by *suffering* the loss of all things.

When I asked my Father to open my understanding of this process of suffering the loss of all things, He answered me by using words of alliteration of the letter *W*. He spoke to me that dying to my carnal life would mean "to give up your *way*, your *wants*, your *works*, your *words*, your *worship*, your *walk* and your *warfare*, and exchange them for Mine."

I began to understand that, without being irreverent, we can think of Calvary as a divine "swap shop." I take my "junk" to the cross, surrender to His will in every area of my life, and exchange it for His divine life. My way is important to me, but it does not bring forth eternal fruit; His way does. Even my worship, which is idolatry of self and other created things, deserves to die so that I can know the true worship of God alone.

What you put into the ground isn't worth much; it needs to die. Even your religious training, as Paul described, will not bring you to Jesus. Paul actually persecuted the church because of his religious training. You may have learned a lot of religious words and Bible stories, and maybe you can even explain theological principles that you have studied. But until the carnal mind is pierced by the Spirit of God and the shell of your outer man crumbles, truth and revelation cannot come forth in resurrection life. Until then, you do not really see Jesus. It was Paul again who explained the reality of personal crucifixion:

> *Dying to your carnal life means to give up your way, your wants, your works, your words, your worship, your walk and your warfare, and exchange them for His.*

> I have been crucified with Christ; and it is no longer I who live, but Christ lives in me; and the life which I now live in the flesh I live by faith in the Son of God, who loved me, and delivered Himself up for me.
>
> —GALATIANS 2:20

Death to self is the spiritual law that allows the life of Christ to live in you. It is the only way to true fruitfulness and living a life that will glorify God. Unless you believe that your natural life has no value in comparison to the life of God within you, you will not choose resurrection life over your natural life. You will love this life too much to exchange it for Christ's resurrection life and power. In order to do that, you must embrace the third law of the dying seed: the *law of hate.*

Chapter 4

THE LAW
OF HATE

*He who loves his life loses it;
and he who hates his life in this world
shall keep it to life eternal.*
—JOHN 12:25

I n Matthew 5:43–47, Jesus taught us the way of
love, radically commanding us to love even our
enemies and to do good to those who mistreat us.
Though we find it difficult to understand how we can
love those who do not love us, as Christians we learn
that God gives grace to us to forgive and to bless even
our enemies. It is a wonderful characteristic of the
love of God that enables us to experience this kind of
supernatural love.

So does Jesus contradict His command for us to
love by telling us to hate? Why does He say, for
example, that "he who hates his life in this world
shall keep it to life eternal" (John 12:25)? In Mark
12:33 He said that we must love our neighbors as we
love ourselves. Are we to love ourselves or hate ourselves? The answer lies in the meaning of the word
hate to which Jesus referred.

When Jesus declared in Luke 14:26 that we cannot
be His disciples unless we hate father, mother,
spouse, children, brothers and sisters—and even our
own life—He was not telling us to feel animosity
toward our families. The Amplified Bible clarifies
His statement by addressing the meaning of the
word in the original language:

> If anyone comes to Me and does not hate his
> [own] father and mother [in the sense of
> indifference to or relative disregard for them
> in comparison with his attitude toward God]
> and [likewise] his wife and children and
> brothers and sisters—[yes] and even his own

life also—he cannot be My disciple.
—LUKE 14:26, AMP

The hatred that Jesus describes is a strong feeling of disregard, but it is not based in animosity or anger. It is felt only in contrast to the strength of love for God and a desire to please Him, which will not allow any other interest or object of love to compete with it. In other words, Jesus taught that if anything else has priority in your affections, you won't see Jesus.

He wasn't teaching not to love father and mother or family and friends. But He was saying that the love for Him would have to be so strong and other loves would be so much less that they would seem like hatred in comparison. It is fair to conclude that if you want to see Jesus, you must want it more than anything else on earth.

As I travel in ministry, I am sensing this deep hunger in people to see Jesus. They are discontent and perplexed, not understanding exactly what is happening to them. When they express their confusion, I shout, "Hallelujah! You are being pressed toward God." This is the best news I have heard regarding the sovereign plan of God for the church.

If you are not discontent, you won't move. If you are not hungry, you won't eat. If you are not being pushed, you won't go. There has been too much apathy in the church, too much religiosity and false contentment with men's programs. Thank God the Holy Spirit is making us uncomfortable just as the mother eagle tears feathers out of her nest to make it uncomfortable when it is time for her eaglets to fly. We must leave other loves behind and long for the only love that will truly satisfy our hearts—love for God alone.

I am not saying that you are not a Christian any more than I would say the eagle's offspring were not little eagles. But unless you are pressed into the life of Christ as those eaglets are pressed into the flight of an eagle, you will lose the higher spiritual life by choosing to remain in the lower, natural life in which you have become comfortable. There is a vast difference in knowing Christ through natural understanding and coming to know His lordship as the apostle Paul did when he declared he had been "crucified with Christ" (Gal. 2:20).

> *The hatred Jesus describes is a strong feeling of disregard. In other words, if anything else has priority in your affections, you won't see Jesus.*

As you embrace the law of hate, you become willing to lay down your thoughts and opinions to think the thoughts of Christ and discover His will for your life. The apostle Paul admonished:

> I beseech you therefore, brethren, by the mercies of God, that ye present your bodies a living sacrifice, holy, acceptable unto God, which

is your reasonable service. And be not conformed to this world: but be ye transformed
by the renewing of your mind, that ye may
prove what is that good, and acceptable, and
perfect, will of God.

—ROMANS 12:1–2, KJV

Here it is again—the picture of death by sacrifice.
Paul teaches that we must present ourselves to God,
which is only our reasonable service, and allow our
minds to be renewed so that we can be transformed
and learn to know the will of God for our lives. His
mind is going to be our mind and His will our will
as we exchange our life for His.

Again, the law of hate is at work, which allows
you to give up your strong opinions and ways of
thinking that oppose God's way. If you love your
carnal mind and pride yourself on your education
and natural wisdom, you love yourself more than
you love Christ. You will not pursue the revelation
of God in your life if you are enamored with the
revelation of your natural intellect. The apostle Paul
had suffered the loss of his great religious learning
and died to the strength of his own intellect in his
pursuit of Christ. To the Corinthian church, which
was a carnal church and enamored with its spiritual
gifts, he declared:

For I determined to know nothing among
you except Jesus Christ, and Him crucified.
And I was with you in weakness and in fear
and in much trembling. And my message and

my preaching were not in persuasive words
of wisdom, but in demonstration of the
Spirit and of power, that your faith should
not rest on the wisdom of men, but on the
power of God.

—1 CORINTHIANS 2:2–5

When Christians attempt to exercise spiritual
gifts without allowing the laws of death to self and
hatred for all that is carnal to work in their natural
lives, they contaminate even the good that God
would accomplish
through the gifts He
has given them. There
is a terrible mixture
of carnality that is
willing to compete
with other brothers
and sisters in the
body of Christ, to
boast of giftings and
be lifted up in pride. It is sad that the life of Christ
cannot be clearly seen by people outside the
church who pass judgment on the love of God
because of the contention and other un-Christlike
behavior they see in the lives of carnal Christians.

If you are not discontent, you won't move. If you are not hungry, you won't eat. If you are not being pushed, you won't go.

So the law of hate must work in our affections,
causing us to seek after Christ with greater fervor
than we would feel for any other relationship. And
it must work in our intellects, making all our
thoughts submit to the law of God and choose to

seek His wisdom rather than our own. It was the apostle James who contrasted the wisdom of this earth with the wisdom of God:

> Who is a wise man and endued with knowledge among you? let him shew out of a good conversation his works with meekness of wisdom. But if ye have bitter envying and strife in your hearts, glory not, and lie not against the truth. This wisdom descendeth not from above, but is earthly, sensual, devilish. For where envying and strife is, there is confusion and every evil work. But the wisdom that is from above is first pure, then peaceable, gentle, and easy to be intreated, full of mercy and good fruits, without partiality, and without hypocrisy.
>
> —JAMES 3:13–17, KJV

Unless you choose to die to your own earthly wisdom, you will continually find your life filled with strife, confusion and every evil work. Only as you allow the wisdom that is from above to replace your wisdom will you enjoy the resurrection power of God in your intellect. The beautiful characteristics of God's wisdom include purity, peace, gentleness, mercy, good fruits, fairness and sincerity. What a powerful exchange is available when you hate your ways and choose the Lord's.

When the apostle Paul prayed for the church at Ephesus, he was praying for every believer in the body of Christ to receive a spirit of wisdom. If you will pray that prayer with your whole heart, God will answer it and give you the desire of your heart, which is His desire for you as well:

> I ... do not cease giving thanks for you, while making mention of you in my prayers; that the God of our Lord Jesus Christ, the Father of glory, may give to you a spirit of wisdom and of revelation in the knowledge of Him. I pray that the eyes of your heart may be enlightened, so that you may know what is the hope of His calling, what are the riches of the glory of His inheritance in the saints, and what is the surpassing greatness of His power toward us who believe.
>
> —EPHESIANS 1:15–19

As I explained earlier, the law of hate simply means to love less in comparison to the love of our lives— Christ Himself. I don't believe we can give up anything that is dear to us unless we learn to hate it—until we see it as He sees it. Whatever habit, sin or unhealthy relationship we cling to will keep us from seeing Jesus until we begin to love it less than we love Him. Even good things that God

As you embrace the law of hate, you become willing to lay down your thoughts and opinions to think the thoughts of Christ and discover His will for your life.

wants us to enjoy can become a stumbling block if we love them more than we love God.

I pray that God will put a hatred in me for anything that keeps me from Him. My plea is similar to the apostle Paul's declaration when he said he suffered the loss of all things "and do count them but dung, that I may win Christ" (Phil. 3:8, KJV). If you came to church and looked down at the altar and saw a deposit of cow dung, you would hurry to remove it—to get rid of it. Paul said he counted all things that he once valued as mere refuse so that he might win Christ

> *Only as you allow the wisdom that is from above to replace your wisdom will you enjoy the resurrection power of God in your intellect.*

Consider the most valuable possession, position or person in your life—someone or something that you feel you could not live without. Could any of these be keeping you from seeing Jesus? Do they occupy a place in your life that is to be reserved for Christ alone? I challenge you to bring them to Jesus and surrender them to His lordship. You will never be sorry for making Jesus first in your life; He will cause everything else you value to take its rightful place, and He will give you the blessing of His presence that you desire.

The Scriptures are filled with instructions to help

us guard our affections so that we can follow Jesus wholeheartedly. Jesus' beloved disciple, John, warned us regarding our relationship to this world:

> Do not love the world, nor the things in the world. If anyone loves the world, the love of the Father is not in him. For all that is in the world, the lust of the flesh and the lust of the eyes and the boastful pride of life, is not from the Father, but is from the world. And the world is passing away, and also its lusts; but the one who does the will of God abides forever.
>
> —1 JOHN 2:15–17

There is no compromise in the Scriptures between your love for God and your relationship with this world. If you find compromise in yourself, you can know that whatever is involved in your loving the world and the things in the world will serve only to keep you from seeing Jesus. Until you can see the things in you that in the eyes of God are as dung, you won't get rid of them. And God said you won't become that productive seed until you first hate the things that compromise your love for God.

If you would see Jesus, you will have to allow the law of hate to work over every area of your life. As you choose to surrender to the element of time in which God arranges circumstances in your life to show you where you love your natural life more than you desire to see Christ's life revealed in you, you must then choose to die to those natural loves.

As you suffer the loss of those things that keep you from Christ, you will learn what it means to be His disciple. The law of discipleship embraces the first three laws of the dying seed: the law of the *time element*, the law of *death* and the law of *hate*.

Chapter 5

THE LAW OF DISCIPLESHIP

If anyone serves Me, let him follow Me;
and where I am, there shall
My servant also be.
—JOHN 12:26

Death to every other love and hatred for life itself will be required if you are going to become a true disciple of Christ. While these may seem harsh requirements for realizing the fulfillment of your heart's desire to see Jesus, they do not come close to the sacrificial requirements that brought Jesus to earth, to become a man and to suffer death, even death on the cross. (See Philippians 2:6–8.)

Can we ever grasp the magnitude of what the incarnation—God becoming man—cost the Son of God, requiring Him to leave the limitless, perfect realm of God to enter the limited, sinful domain of mankind? Perhaps the revelation the apostle Paul had of this *kenosis* (emptying) of the Godhead enabled him to suffer the loss of all things in order to win Christ:

> Have this attitude in yourselves which was also in Christ Jesus, who, although He existed in the form of God, did not regard equality with God a thing to be grasped, but emptied Himself, taking the form of a bond-servant, and being made in the likeness of men. And being found in appearance as a man, He humbled Himself by becoming obedient to the point of death, even death on a cross.
>
> —PHILIPPIANS 2:5–8

Here is the attitude we must adopt toward our own "emptying" of our self life if we are to follow Jesus and become His disciple and His servant. If the Son of God did not hesitate to relinquish His

"equality with God" to take the form of a bond servant as a man, and if He could humble Himself
further to the point
of death on a cross,
surely we can be
Death to every other
love and hatred for life
itself will be required
if you are going to
become a true disciple
of Christ.
inspired by such great
love to give up all we
hold dear to enter
into relationship with
Him. Following Jesus
doesn't mean simply
striving to under-
stand and obey His
teachings; it involves loving Him enough to go
where He goes and to become a servant as He
became a servant.

The law of discipleship is not difficult to understand, although it may be difficult to embrace. As I
mentioned in the last chapter, it will require the *law of*
the time element, the *law of death* and the *law of hate* to
be working in your life in order for you to fulfill the
law of discipleship.

What does it mean to be a disciple? By definition,
a *disciple* is a "learner" or "one who is taught." In the
New Testament *disciple* is the rendering of the Greek
word *mathetes*; it applies to one who professes to
have learned certain principles from another and
maintains them on that other's authority. It is
applied principally to the followers of Jesus.[1] A willingness to be taught and an openness to learn the

ways of Christ are basic requirements for becoming a disciple.

CHARACTERISTICS OF A DISCIPLE

There are several characteristics of a disciple of Jesus that you can recognize in your life when you are embracing the law of discipleship. Discipleship is not a state of being but rather a journey into relationship with your Lord, Jesus Christ. These are elements that will be a necessary part of the journey for you to arrive at your destination, which is to see Jesus in all of His glory.

Supreme love for Jesus Christ

As I stated in the chapter on the law of hate, there can be no other love competing with our love for Christ if we are to be His disciples. Too often our desire to see Jesus is tempered by our desires for other things. On one occasion, when Jesus was addressing the issue of discipleship, He told a parable to illustrate the cost involved:

> For which one of you, when he wants to build a tower, does not first sit down and calculate the cost, to see if he has enough to complete it? Otherwise, when he has laid a foundation, and is not able to finish, all who observe it begin to ridicule him, saying, "This man began to build and was not able to finish." ... So therefore, no one of you can be My disciple who does not give up all his own possessions.
>
> —LUKE 14:28–30, 33

To follow Jesus you must be willing to be radical, to make it obvious that He has priority over everything else that you consider to be a part of your life.

> Following Jesus involves loving Him enough to go where He goes and to become a servant as He became a servant.

And not just for the short term—it is to be the case for the entire journey, lest you start something and not be able to finish it. Sadly, in my years of ministry, I have seen too many sincere believers enthusiastically declare that they wanted to be disciples of Christ without determining to count the cost and make Him Lord of all.

Many have not been willing to give up some possession or position that was dear to them, or a relationship that meant more to them than their relationship with the Lord. There is nothing or no one that is worthy to keep us from knowing Christ and becoming His disciple wholeheartedly. They can only cheat us out of the one prize that is worth giving our whole life to receive—an intimate relationship with the Lord of all.

Does Christ expect us to live without possessions, positions or relationships? No. But He does expect them to be surrendered to His lordship and handled loosely in our affections, never taking the place He deserves as Lord of our lives. Only as we dare to abandon ourselves to God can we enjoy the things of this earth without becoming wrongly attached to them. Even the blessings of God can become a curse to us if they take the wrong place in our affections, robbing us of the most valuable treasure of all—our destiny in the kingdom of God.

Jesus illustrated the worth of the kingdom by telling a parable of a man who was seeking for the greatest treasure of all:

> The kingdom of heaven is like a treasure hidden in the field, which a man found and hid; and from joy over it he goes and sells all that he has, and buys that field.
>
> —MATTHEW 13:44

There was not a sense of agony or sadness, but expressed joy, in this man as he chose to sell everything to buy, not just the treasure, but the entire field where the treasure was buried. Perhaps it is significant to our search for the treasure to understand that the man purchased the field. Sometimes we have to "buy" territory around the treasure in order to get the treasure, even though that territory may seem worthless to us. We must be willing to sell all and buy the field, if necessary, in order to acquire what is truly valuable in the kingdom of God.

When you really glimpse the Master and realize that He can be your "Treasure" to have and to hold, you will not consider it a great sacrifice to give up all you have to receive Him. Becoming a disciple of the Lord means that you love Him above all because He is worthy of your love. His love is not to be compared with any lesser interest you would ever have to forgo.

Denial of self

Self-love is stubborn; it is a hindrance to discipleship. While we may find we can give up all other loves to follow Jesus and become His disciples, we may wince when He touches some thing in our lives that reveals our *self*-love. Our personal identity is dearer to us than we may realize; most of us have spent much of our life developing it and striving to "be" somebody.

> *You must be willing to be radical, to make it obvious that Christ has priority over everything else that you consider to be a part of your life.*

As we choose to die to our self-interests, we are allowing the "seed" of our life to fall into the ground where the "natural" elements do their work to loosen the outer shell of our self life and release the supernatural life of God that is within us. Some refer to this as the work of sanctification or cleansing of the Christian. I wish I could say it is an instantaneous work, as some believe. I was taught that sanctification, the death of the old man and the perfection of the new creation, could be an instantaneous happening. The only problem with that doctrine was that it didn't work.

I have come to believe that there is a beautiful doctrine of sanctification that does involve a commitment, a total surrender to the lordship of Christ at a specific time. We can point to the place where we built an altar and put our self life on it, choosing to die to our self-interests and to follow Christ. But I also believe that every new epoch in life calls for a new memorial. We don't just build one altar; we keep building them and surrendering our self life to the flames as we progress in our journey of discipleship.

We dig new wells to receive revelation of the Word of God that continually washes us. I believe that you track saints by watching where they built altars and where they dug wells. Every new altar and freshly dug well means you live less for yourself and more in God. The Scriptures teach us to reckon ourselves dead to sin:

> Likewise reckon ye also yourselves to be dead
> indeed unto sin, but alive unto God through
> Jesus Christ our Lord.
>
> —ROMANS 6:11, KJV

The Greek word for *reckon (logizomai)* means "to conclude or take account of," showing us how to think about our noninvolvement in sin.[2] We are to take inventory of our lives and determine to be dead to sin. As we do so, we come into agreement with the Holy Spirit who dwells in us and is working to conform us to the image of Christ. We cannot change ourselves. Our part is simply to agree with God, reckon ourselves dead and allow our faith to embrace His holiness within.

My little granddaughter used to say "plyke" for "play like." She would say to me in her childish insistence, "Grandma, let's plyke!" In a sense, that is what we do with our self life. We "plyke" it doesn't live there any more; we reckon ourselves dead to sin. Did you ever look in the mirror and say to yourself, "Who asked you?" When you are struggling with an issue in your walk with God, tell yourself, "You don't get a vote. Dead people don't vote." We have to act like we are dead to the self life that hinders our discipleship, and then the power of God will make that a reality.

> *Sometimes we have to "buy" territory around the treasure in order to get the treasure.*

Abiding in the Word

It is impossible to be a disciple of Christ without an unswerving dedication to the Word of God. Jesus declared that we must abide in Him, the living Word, as branches abide in a vine in order to have His life in us:

> Abide in Me, and I in you. As the branch cannot bear fruit of itself, unless it abides in the vine, so neither can you, unless you abide in Me...If you abide in Me, and My words abide

in you, ask whatever you wish, and it shall be
done for you.

—JOHN 15:4, 7

If you understand who Christ is, you will know
why you must learn to abide in the written Word to
have His life within you. The apostle John recognized Christ as the living Word that came from
heaven:

> In the beginning was the Word, and the Word
> was with God, and the Word was God. The
> same was in the beginning with God. All
> things were made by him; and without him
> was not any thing made that was made. In him
> was life; and the life was the light of men.
>
> —JOHN 1:1–4, KJV

While I cannot discuss in-depth the wonder of
this mystery here, you need to be clear about the fact
that because Christ is the living Word, you cannot
hope to know Him—to see Him—if you do not
meditate on the written Word. As the Holy Spirit
becomes your Teacher, He will reveal Jesus to you
through the written Word. Jesus Himself promised
that "when He, the Spirit of truth, comes, He will
guide you into all the truth…He shall glorify Me; for
He shall take of Mine, and shall disclose it to you"
(John 16:13–14).

The Scriptures declare that the Word of God
came to us through holy men who were moved
upon by the Holy Spirit. (See 2 Peter 1:21.) In his

epistle, James tells us how to be cleansed from all uncleanness:

> So get rid of all uncleanness and the rampant outgrowth of wickedness, and in a humble (gentle, modest) spirit receive and welcome the Word which implanted and rooted [in your hearts] contains the power to save your souls.
>
> —JAMES 1:21, AMP

The Word of God contains the power to save us. It is imperative that we become thoroughly acquainted with it and continually give ourselves to its study. James goes on to warn us not to be hearers of the Word only, but to obey it so that we do not become deceived. (See James 1:22.) As disciples of Christ, we must embrace the Word of God, learning its precepts and submitting our wills to obey them. Without the Word of God, we will not have faith to follow Christ or obey His commands. The Scriptures clearly teach, "Faith comes from hearing, and hearing by the word of Christ" (Rom. 10:17).

When you are struggling with an issue in your walk with God, tell your self, "You don't get a vote. Dead people don't vote."

Even before Christ came to earth, Old Testament saints knew the key to success for life:

> This book of the law shall not depart out of thy

> mouth; but thou shalt meditate therein
> day and night, that thou mayest observe to do
> according to all that is written therein: for
> then thou shalt make thy way prosperous,
> and then thou shalt have good success.
>
> —JOSHUA 1:8, KJV

Meditation for Christians seems to be a lost art—lost to continual activity and "noise-makers" like TVs, car radios, stereos and other gadgets that shut out the silence necessary to help us meditate. But the biblical injunction to meditate on the law of God has not changed. We need to read the Word and then consider its application to our lives.

When we go to the grocery store or drive to work, we can *selah*—pause and think about—what we have read. Somewhat like Bessie the cow who eats the green grass and then lies down under a tree but continues to chew her cud, we need to continually feed on the living truths of the Scriptures, asking the Holy Spirit to apply them to our lives.

The apostle Paul understood the cleansing power of the Word of God when He wrote:

> …Christ also loved the church and gave
> Himself up for her; that He might sanctify her,
> having cleansed her by the washing of water
> with the word, that He might present to
> Himself the church in all her glory, having no
> spot or wrinkle or any such thing; but that she
> should be holy and blameless.
>
> —EPHESIANS 5:25–27

Paul also instructed believers to "lay aside the old self, which is being corrupted in accordance with the lusts of deceit, and that you be renewed in the spirit of your mind" (Eph. 4:22–23). Neglecting the Word of God will result in several defeating scenarios:

- ∾ You will grow weary. The Scriptures teach that health and strength come to us through the precepts of God. (See Proverbs 3.)

- ∾ You will become unhappy. Losing perspective of true values, the heart and mind quickly form attachments with things that cannot satisfy.

- ∾ You can be led into deception easily. Sadly, many ministers who have fallen into sin have admitted their lack of prayer and reading of the Word. They said that if they had been in the Word and in prayer, they would never have fallen.

- ∾ You begin to neglect the assembly of believers. Church attendance and involvement with the body of Christ do not seem important when you do not continue to see the purposes of God revealed for His church in the Word of God.

If you expect to be successful in your journey of discipleship, you will need to make the Word of God a priority in your life, heeding the warnings of the Scriptures to obey it, love it and meditate on it day and night. Indeed, love for the Word of God can be equated with love for God Himself.

Love for one another

Jesus gave some poignant instructions to His disciples during His last supper with them. He declared:

> A new commandment I give to you, that you love one another, even as I have loved you, that you also love one another. By this all men will know that you are My disciples, if you have love for one another.
>
> —JOHN 13:34–35

One of my professors was an elderly, silver-haired man who was one of the godliest men I have ever known. One day he read to us from 1 Corinthians 13—the love chapter—and all of us students were in tears just listening to him read it. Then he led the way to the altar, tears streaming down his own cheeks. The apostle Paul was describing in that chapter the love of God, not our love, that we can allow to flow through us to others.

Because Christ is the living Word, you cannot hope to know Him if you do not meditate on the written Word.

The more you love Christ and desire to be His disciple, the more love you will have for others. As you yield to the Holy Spirit, He pours out His love in your heart, as Paul wrote about in Romans 5:5, and you are able to love even the unlovely. God's love is unconditional. It is universal; it is complete. You cannot love God without loving His family.

When Jesus told the disciples to love one another the way He had loved them, I think they knew what He meant. We can be sure that He loved each of His disciples unconditionally. It is probably safe to say they did not share that depth of love for each other, especially since we know that this love is supernatural—it comes from God Himself. Jesus was giving them a command to love each other as He had loved them. It must have seemed impossible to them. Yet He continued His instructions, declaring that in this way the world would know they were Jesus' disciples—by their love for one another. Not by the miracles they performed or the great teaching ministries they developed. Love would be the identifying characteristic of Jesus' disciples—unconditional love for the brethren. And it is still the identifying characteristic today.

> *The more you love Christ and desire to be His disciple, the more love you will have for others.*

of seven hundred grains on it. One grain of corn is expected to reap four times seven hundred grains, or twenty-eight hundred grains of corn. If those twenty-eight hundred grains of corn are replanted—you do the math to understand the law of multiplication that is working in the harvest.

In every apple there is a seed that, if properly planted, holds promise of reproduction.

When Jesus taught the parable of the sower, He held out the promise of bringing forth one hundredfold in harvest:

> But he that received seed into the good ground is he that heareth the word, and understandeth it; which also beareth fruit, and bringeth forth, some an hundredfold, some sixty, some thirty.
>
> —MATTHEW 13:23, KJV

When Peter wanted to know how God runs His government, he said to Jesus, "Behold, we have left everything and followed You; what then will there be for us?" (Matt. 19:27). Jesus' response revealed the law of the harvest, the promise of fruitfulness that could be expected from a "dying seed":

> And every one that hath forsaken houses, or brethren, or sisters, or father, or mother, or wife, or children, or lands, for my name's sake,

shall receive an hundredfold, and shall inherit
everlasting life.

—MATTHEW 19:29, KJV

I believe Jesus was promising fruitfulness and
harvest that would take all eternity to receive to the
full. It is impossible to calculate a hundredfold of
God's blessings, along with the promise of everlasting life. Without a dying seed, there will be no harvest. But when the seed falls into the ground to die,
surrendering all to the lordship of Christ, a harvest
is inevitable.

Fruitfulness is the characteristic of a disciple
that brings benefit to others. You have been given
life—eternal life—that you might share that life with
others. Jesus said, "You are the salt of the earth...You
are the light of the world" (Matt. 5:13–14). These
attributes of a true disciple are attributes

Discipleship is not an instant experience; it involves growth and development.

that people without God desperately need. For
example, salt has wonderful preservation proper-
ties, and light dispels darkness. As you abide in the
Word, you can speak into lives truth that will be
redemptive, helping others to turn to the light and
become disciples of Christ. Your love for Christ
will shine forth and draw others to Him.

EMBRACING THE CROSS

Discipleship is not an instant experience; it involves growth and development. You don't get it all at once. A true disciple is continually becoming more fully a disciple—one who learns and then practices what he learns.

In this chapter I described a disciple as one who has a supreme love for Jesus, denies himself, abides in the Word, loves others as he loves himself and lives a life of fruitfulness. None of this is possible without embracing the cross life.

There is no mystery to what the cross means in a believer's life. It is simply that wherever my will or desires oppose the will of God, that place becomes a cross for me. If I choose my own will, I have not embraced the cross. If I choose the will of God, it crosses my will, and I must choose to die to what I want in order to embrace the will of God.

After I had preached the word for seventeen years, I became gravely ill and was told by physicians that I would die. But friends took me to a Pentecostal church where the Lord healed me and baptized me in the Holy Spirit.[3] Those supernatural experiences set me on a new path of revelation of the Word of God. For months afterward, I began to hear a question in my spirit that bothered me—a question that I wrestled with.

The Holy Spirit was asking me, "How deep can the cross penetrate into you?" It seemed as if I could see

someone laying a cross on me and pressing it into me.
I remembered that the furniture Moses placed in the
tabernacle by the command of God was situated in
the shape of a cross. And I knew the Scriptures called
us tabernacles, or temples, of God. (See 1 Corinthians
3:16.) God wants to place the cross deeply into our
spirits in order to bring death to our self life and
release His resurrection life in us. As we die to our
thoughts, the mind of Christ becomes ours; we die to
our works and begin to do His.

How deep can the cross penetrate into your life? If
you choose to live in the cross, it becomes a way of
life. It is not just an instrument of death; it is the way
to resurrection life. The apostle Paul understood this
journey to true discipleship when he declared:

> I have been crucified with Christ; and it is no
> longer I who live, but Christ lives in me; and
> the life which I now live in the flesh I live by
> faith in the Son of God, who loved me, and
> delivered Himself up for me.
>
> —GALATIANS 2:20

There will always be a cross in true discipleship; it
is on the pathway of our deliberate choice to follow
Jesus. Sometimes that brings abuse and criticism
from others who do not understand our choices. We
seem to be going in an opposite direction from the
way family and friends are going. However, the cross
is the path to fruitfulness and resurrection life and
power—and our goal to see Jesus.

If you are still reading and choosing to embrace

the five laws of the dying seed in order to reach your goal to see Jesus, you are well on your way to the unspeakable joy of knowing Jesus as Lord and fulfilling your eternal destiny.

As we discuss the fifth law, that of *identification* with Him, understand that, while there are some requirements involved here as well, the synergy that is working in your life through the previous laws is creating the environment for your identification with the Master already. Your goal is certain; you will not be disappointed.

> "How deep can the cross penetrate into you?"

Chapter 6

THE LAW OF IDENTIFICATION

…Christ in you, the hope of glory.
—COLOSSIANS 1:27

When I get to the subject of identification with Christ, I feel overwhelmed with awe of the wonderful revelation He has given us to walk in. I walked with God and even taught the Word for many years before I had any revelation of the *law of identification* that death to self works in us. As an evangelist and pastor, I worked so hard for the Lord and tried to follow Him, making His life the pattern for mine. My theological studies had taught me to try to live *as* He did. My professors would paint a wonderful picture of the attributes of God; then they taught us to try to duplicate them in our lives.

Unfortunately, when we try to do that in our own strength, we begin to live under the bondage of legalism, keeping rules and laws without understanding the grace of God that must be released in our lives through identification with Christ in His death. For years I tried to be holy and righteous. Whatever my leaders said would accomplish that goal, I adhered to. There were many external dos and don'ts that were supposed to indicate whether or not we were living like Christ. For years I didn't drink coffee or Coke; I didn't cut my hair or wear red because the church said these things were sinful. I wanted to follow Jesus, so I obeyed these external rules of the church, thinking I was pleasing God.

After I was healed and filled with the Holy Spirit, I attended a conference in Canada. I was listening to the message being preached, and suddenly my Teacher, the Holy Spirit, let me hear, "I have become your righteousness and sanctification." He revealed to me the wonderful promise of 1 Corinthians 1:30–31:

> But by His doing you are in Christ Jesus, who became to us wisdom from God, and right-eousness and sanctification, and redemption, that, just as it is written, "Let him who boasts, boast in the LORD."

In that moment I understood that I didn't work *for* Christ; He works *in* me and *through* me. I knew that I didn't live *for* Him; I live *in* Him. I also understood that following Jesus did not mean trying to walk as He did, but allowing Him to live in me. I began to weep with relief and joy in the revealed truth that was liberating me from so much legalism in which I had struggled to do in my own strength what only His divine life could do. As I sat in that service, I had a glimpse of Jesus, the wonderful Savior who desired to live His life through me and make me holy and righteous with His righteousness. In an instant, it seemed as if years of weariness melted away, and I understood Jesus' invitation:

We don't work for Christ; He works in us and through us. We don't live for Christ; we live in Him.

> Come unto me, all ye that labour and are
> heavy laden, and I will give you rest. Take my
> yoke upon you, and learn of me; for I am
> meek and lowly in heart: and ye shall find rest
> unto your souls. For my yoke is easy, and my
> burden is light.
>
> —MATTHEW 11:28–30

I began to understand that the law of identification worked in my heart from the moment I received Christ as Savior and Lord, setting me free from sin and self—judicially. My part was not to try to live for Him or work for Him, but to *yield* to Him and allow the divine life of God within to be released through me.

When the minister finished his sermon, the congregation sang the old spiritual "Were You There?", which walked us through the crucifixion, burial and resurrection of the Lord. As I listened, instead of watching those awful events happen to Jesus, it was as if I were on the cross with Him…buried with Him …and raised with Him. That wonderful revelation of my identification with Christ in His death, burial and resurrection has been transforming my life ever since I understood what the apostle Paul declared:

> And when you were dead in your transgressions and the uncircumcision of your flesh, He made you alive together with Him, having forgiven us all our transgressions, having canceled out the certificate of debt consisting of decrees against us and which was hostile to us;

and He has taken it out of the way, having
nailed it to the cross.

—Colossians 2:13–14

While I knew I had been forgiven my sins and had
preached His saving grace to many, the wonderful
position I had attained in Christ, through no efforts
of my own, was just dawning in my spirit. To the
Ephesians, Paul explained:

> But God, who is rich in mercy, for his great
> love wherewith he loved us, even when we
> were dead in sins, hath quickened us together
> with Christ, (by grace ye are saved;) and hath
> raised us up together, and made us sit together
> in heavenly places in Christ Jesus.

—Ephesians 2:4–6, kjv

Right now, according to the Scriptures, I am
seated with Christ in heavenly places. My home is in God. My inner man is already in eternity. I am saved by grace, not by anything I will ever do for Christ or to become holy. Needless to say, I have enjoyed a cup of coffee or a Coke occasionally ever since. Not only that, but I have walked in a security in Christ and a freedom to trust Him as my

The law of identification represents the bursting forth of the new life that was resident in the seed when it went into the ground.

righteousness and my sanctification that I did not know existed. He is becoming my all in all.

The law of identification represents the bursting forth of the new life that was resident in the seed when it went into the ground. The seed has submitted to the law of the time element, the law of death, the law of hate and the law of discipleship. All of these forces have burst open the hard shell of the seed to reveal the precious life of God that has been developing under the soil, out of the sight of everyone except the Master Husbandman. The fruit is coming forth in the reality of "Christ in you, the hope of glory" (Col. 1:27).

One day after I had returned home from that conference in Canada, I was traveling in Atlanta and was stuck in traffic because of an accident. As I sat there, the Holy Spirit continued to teach me my lesson of identification with Christ. I heard Him whisper to me, "You in me; I in you; Christ in you; you in Christ; God in Christ; Christ in God; Christ in the Holy Spirit; the Holy Spirit in Christ." Then He asked me, "How do you like your position?"

I responded, "I am beginning to like it a lot, but I am not sure I understand. Please help me to understand."

He told me to get my sand bucket. I told Him I didn't own a sand bucket. But in my imagination, I went to get my young son's sand bucket. Then the Holy Spirit showed me the Pacific Ocean. He said, "Go get some of the ocean in your bucket." So, like a child, I obeyed and filled my bucket with ocean water. Then He asked me, "What do you have in your bucket?"

I replied, "The ocean."

He said, "Look again at the ocean. Which would you rather have, the ocean in your bucket or the Pacific Ocean?"

I answered, "The Pacific Ocean."

He then told me, "Then go jump in, bucket and all."

That simple illustration taught me that, although I had every element of the ocean in my "bucket," it was only a small part of the ocean. But as I abandoned myself to the ocean, I could have all its power rush over me and carry me along. I understood more clearly how identification with God Himself transcends my little "bucket" of life, though He does dwell there.

> God is our light, life, wisdom and righteousness—all we need to experience the resurrection life of Christ.

The Scriptures teach that the life of Christ in us is a "treasure in earthen vessels, that the excellency of the power may be of God, and not of us" (2 Cor 4:7, KJV). That is the resurrection life that bursts forth from the dying seed, having embraced the laws of God that are certain to bring forth life. Eternity is already in us. Not one thing that our inner man needs can we get from this world. God is our light, life, wisdom and righteousness—all we need to experience the resurrection life of Christ. Paul declared, "In Him all the fulness of Deity dwells in bodily form, and in Him you have been made complete" (Col. 2:9–10). That comes as a result of taking the death route.

Embracing the law of identification doesn't mean God annihilates me. The apostle Paul declared:

> I have been crucified with Christ; and it is no longer I who live, but Christ lives in me; and the life which I now live in the flesh I live by faith in the Son of God, who loved me, and delivered Himself up for me.
>
> —GALATIANS 2:20

You live in the flesh, furnishing a house or temple for Christ to live in. As you yield to the law of identification, Christ lives His life through you.

Without yielding to the law of identification with Christ working in you, you depend on your works—earning your way to heaven. Without the divine seed in you bringing forth resurrection life, you will never be able to live the Christ life. Christian character is formed in the seed that has abandoned itself to the ground; it is supernatural power that forms the divine nature in you. It will never be attained by the efforts of the flesh to "do better."

Only as His Word germinates in you do you bring forth the fruit and life that glorify Him. Just as you

cannot bring forth resurrection life without dying,
the converse is also true: You cannot die to self without bringing forth life. It is a law. Death is only
worked in the outer shell of the seed; life springs
forth from within. And the more you die to your old
self life, the more Christ lives His life through you.
The apostle Paul understood this process when he
instructed believers:

> I urge you therefore, brethren, by the mercies
> of God, to present your bodies a living and
> holy sacrifice, acceptable to God, which is your
> spiritual service of worship. And do not be
> conformed to this world, but be transformed
> by the renewing of your mind, that you may
> prove what the will of God is, that which is
> good and acceptable and perfect.
>
> —ROMANS 12:1–2

Transformation is the result of embracing the
laws of the dying seed. The goal of death is life—
resurrection life that is totally identified with
Christ. Our minds and hearts are renewed by the
washing of the Word and obedience to the will of
God. Our sinful character gives way to the wonderful divine nature of God. It was Peter who declared
this reality so powerfully:

> Grace and peace be multiplied to you in
> the knowledge of God and of Jesus our Lord;
> seeing that His divine power has granted
> to us everything pertaining to life and
> godliness, through the true knowledge of

Him who called us by His own glory and
excellence.

—2 PETER 1:2–3

If anyone in the Scriptures demonstrates the
transforming power of God in his life, it is Peter.
Bold and blustering, filled with self-confidence
before Christ's death, Peter declared he would go
with Christ to His death, only to discover how bit-
terly deceived he was
about the weakness of
his own flesh. He
denied even knowing
Christ and was filled
with shame after-
wards. We can easily
relate to the weak-
nesses of Peter—
many times we think

> *Just as you cannot bring
> forth resurrection life
> without dying, you
> cannot die to self without
> bringing forth life.*

we can do something wonderful for God only to fail
miserably. In that painful place we can receive
greater revelation of the utter weakness of our flesh,
which will cause us to yield to the Holy Spirit, who
will bring forth His life.

On the Day of Pentecost, when Peter stood up to
preach and three thousand souls were saved, we see
a man empowered by the Holy Spirit, transformed
from the coward of a few days earlier. When he wrote
his epistles as an old man, it is clear that he had
learned to rely on God's divine power, which gave
him—and has given us—everything pertaining to

life and godliness. Gone is the self-confidence; in its place is a new identification with His Lord, Jesus Christ.

The humiliation of Peter's proud boasting was a devastating blow to his pride. It is necessary to receive this kind of blow to our proud hearts in order for the hard shell of the seed to be broken. Usually through some crisis or painful event we discover the weakness of our flesh—our self life—and its utter impotence to bring forth the resurrection life of God we desire to produce.

Perhaps the greatest key to being able to see Jesus, as the Greeks in John 12:20–21 desired to do, is humility. I have waited until now to suggest it so that you would have a context into which to place this vital truth. It takes humility to come to Jesus in the first place. The proud heart does not seek God, as the Scriptures plainly declare:

> The wicked, through the pride of his counte-
> nance, will not seek after God: God is not in all
> his thoughts.
> —PSALM 10:4, KJV

The first step toward Christ is a step of humility. Even though Christ is God and therefore could not ever have sinned in pride, the Scriptures declare that "He humbled Himself by becoming obedient to the point of death, even death on a cross" (Phil. 2:8). This same passage begins by admonishing believers to "have this attitude in yourselves which was also in

Christ Jesus" (v. 5). The willingness to abandon yourself to the will of God requires a humbling process for all who would become a "dying seed."

Andrew Murray, in his powerful book *Humility*, defines humility for us:

> Humility means the giving up of self and becoming perfect nothingness before God. Jesus humbled Himself and became obedient unto death. In death He gave the highest, the perfect proof of having given up His will to the will of God. In death He gave up His self, with its natural reluctance to drink the cup. Humility leads to perfect death.[1]

Because of Jesus' humbling, God has exalted Him above every name that is named in heaven and earth. (See Philippians 2:9.) In contrast, Lucifer, who tried to exalt himself above the throne of God and become like the most high God, was cast out of heaven and is doomed to eternal damnation. (See Isaiah 14:12–15.)

The first step toward Christ is a step of humility.

How desperately we need to guard our own hearts against that universal desire to self-exaltation, which attempts to make us a "god" that controls our own destinies.

Embracing the laws of the dying seed not only assures you that you will see Jesus, but it also protects you from the wickedness of proud flesh that does not allow you to seek God. Refusing to seek God means refusing life—the eternal life that Christ has promised. It is imperative that you continually abandon yourself to the processes of the dying seed in order to be set free from your self life that militates against the life of God.

The apostle Paul declared that the carnal mind is hostile against God:

> For the mind set on the flesh is death, but the mind set on the Spirit is life and peace, because the mind set on the flesh is hostile toward God; for it does not subject itself to the law of God, for it is not even able to do so; and those who are in the flesh cannot please God.
>
> —ROMANS 8:6–8

This understanding of the flesh, represented by the hard shell of the seed, makes it imperative that we decide to follow Jesus. Allowing Him to do His precious work in our hearts will remove the shell of our hostility to God and enable us to subject ourselves to the laws of God. If we do not embrace the laws of the dying seed, we will abide alone, in death. The writer of Proverbs declared, "There is a way which seems right to a man, but its end is the way of death" (Prov. 14:12).

That reality narrows your options: Either you abide in death—alone—or you abandon yourself to the will of God, who works death over your flesh in order to bring you forth into resurrection life and power. James declared, "Humble yourselves in the presence of the Lord, and He will exalt you" (James 4:10). And Peter admonished all believers to "clothe yourselves with humility toward one another, for God is opposed to the proud, but gives grace to the humble. Humble yourselves, therefore, under the mighty hand of God, that He may exalt you at the proper time" (1 Pet. 5:5–6).

The five laws of the dying seed expressed in Jesus' discourse that day will never fail to bring the results Jesus promised. Yielding to the *law of the time element* in your life requires humility that refuses to take things into your own hands. Waiting on God to fulfill His purposes in His time causes death to work over your own agenda and personal ambitions.

The *law of death* involves abandonment to the will of God in every area of your life. You may feel you have died to self completely in one area of your life, while another area is just being revealed that requires your surrender to the lordship of Christ. This dying process will continually yield greater fruit as you begin to experience the resurrection life of Jesus.

The *law of hate* must be firmly planted within your minds and hearts to keep you from becoming entangled again in the world and your own carnal desires. Firm goals to pursue your destiny in God and a heavenly perspective are required to allow this law to fully execute its life-giving power within you.

The apostle Paul admonished the Colossians, "If then you have been raised up with Christ, keep seeking the things above, where Christ is, seated at the right hand of God. Set your mind on the things above, not on the things that are on earth" (Col. 3:1–2).

The *law of discipleship* will ever take you more readily into servanthood no matter what your position or the task at hand. When Jesus girded a towel during His last supper with His disciples and began to wash their feet, they were astonished at His actions. But Jesus taught them to do the same to one another and to become a servant of all.

> *Allowing Jesus to do His precious work in our hearts will remove the shell of our hostility to God and enable us to subject ourselves to the laws of God.*

The *law of identification* must be a revelation to your spirit before it can be a reality expressed in your life. You must understand the supernatural work of grace that Christ is doing in your life through salvation in order to enable you to die to self and allow His life to flow through you. The wonderful liberty that comes from giving up your efforts to serve Him and allow Him to live in you is part of the resurrection life that He promises.

Listen to Jesus' words once more as you meditate

on the meaning of the laws of the dying seed. It is my prayer that desire for the beauty of the resurrection life of Jesus will explode into your heart and mind much as the living plant bursts up through the soil where it has been buried and experienced a kind of death:

> And Jesus answered them, saying, "The hour has come for the Son of Man to be glorified. Truly, truly, I say to you, unless a grain of wheat falls into the earth and dies, it remains by itself alone; but if it dies, it bears much fruit. He who loves his life loses it; and he who hates his life in this world shall keep it to life eternal. If anyone serves Me, let him follow Me; and where I am, there shall My servant also be; if anyone serves Me, the Father will honor him."
>
> —JOHN 12:23–26

Amen—so be it.

Notes

Chapter 2
The Law of the Time Element

1. *Matthew Henry's Commentary on the Whole Bible: New Modern Edition, Electronic Database.* Copyright © 1991 by Hendrickson Publishers, Inc., s.v. "John 12:20–26."
2. Ibid.

Chapter 3
The Law of Death

1. *Biblesoft's New Exhaustive Strong's Numbers and Concordance with Expanded Greek-Hebrew Dictionary.* Copyright © 1994, Biblesoft and International Bible Translators, Inc., s.v. "*doxazo.*"
2. James Strong, ed., *The New Strong's Exhaustive Concordance of the Bible* (Nashville: Thomas Nelson, 1997), s.v. "*psuche.*"
3. Ibid., s.v. "*zoe.*"

Chapter 5
The Law of Discipleship

1. Merrill F. Unger, ed., *The New Unger's Bible Dictionary* (Chicago: Moody Press, 1988), s.v. "disciple."
2. *Biblesoft's New Exhaustive Strong's Numbers and Concordance with Expanded Greek-Hebrew Dictionary.* Copyright © 1994, Biblesoft and International Bible Translators, Inc., s.v. "*logizomai.*"

3. You can read more of my testimony in my book *Stones of Remembrance* (Lake Mary, FL: Charisma House, 1998).

CHAPTER 6
THE LAW OF IDENTIFICATION

1. Andrew Murray, *Humility* (Springdale, PA: Whitaker House, 1982), 74–75.

Enjoy your journey with God!

Dr. Fuchsia Pickett has been referred to as one of the "best Bible teachers of our time," and now you know why!

We pray that you have been inspired with the life message found in *Five Laws of the Dying Seed* and we know you'll enjoy two more opportunities to sit under her anointed teaching and draw closer to God.

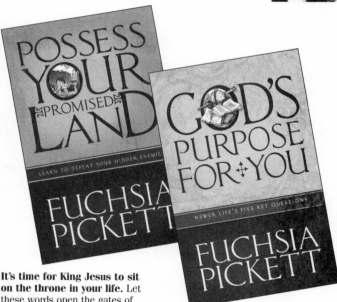

It's time for King Jesus to sit on the throne in your life. Let these words open the gates of your soul through obedience and unlock the gates of your spirit with faith.

Uncover the real meaning of servanthood. Fulfill your purpose and give thanks for everything God has done, all He is doing now, as well as what He is going to do your future.

Everything good starts here!

Call 800-599-5750
Visit your local Christian bookstore
Or order online at charismahouse.com